HORSES MAKE ME LAUGH

Journal

by **Joanne Langford**

What A Beautiful Horse
Publications,
Didsbury AB CA

Horses Make Me Laugh Journal
Published by What A Beautiful Horse in 2019
First edition; First printing

Design and writing ©2019 Joanne Langford
Graphics: Juan Carlo Villarroel
Layout: Joanne Langford
Writing and Editing: Sandy Smith

Images purchased from Shutterstock.com

Facebook: What A Beautiful Horse

ISBN: 978-1-7770330-0-2

Dedication

This book is dedicated to my siblings.
When I see these pictures I am reminded of when
we gave our horse Mame the bread with peanut
butter on it. We laughed for days about that.
I hope that this journal brings back memories and
makes you laugh at the same time.
I love you all very much, I hope you know that.
Thank you for loving me.

Joanne

This Journal belongs to:

____

A lover of horses.

____

If you wish to glimpse inside a human soul and get to know the person, don't bother analyzing their ways of being silent, of talking, of weeping, or seeing how much they are moved by noble ideas; you'll get better results if you just watch them laugh. If they laugh well, they are good people… All I claim to know is that laughter is the most reliable gauge of human nature.

Feodor Dostoyevsky

Wherever man has left his footprint in the long ascent from barbarism to civilization we will find the hoofprint of the horse beside it.

John Moore

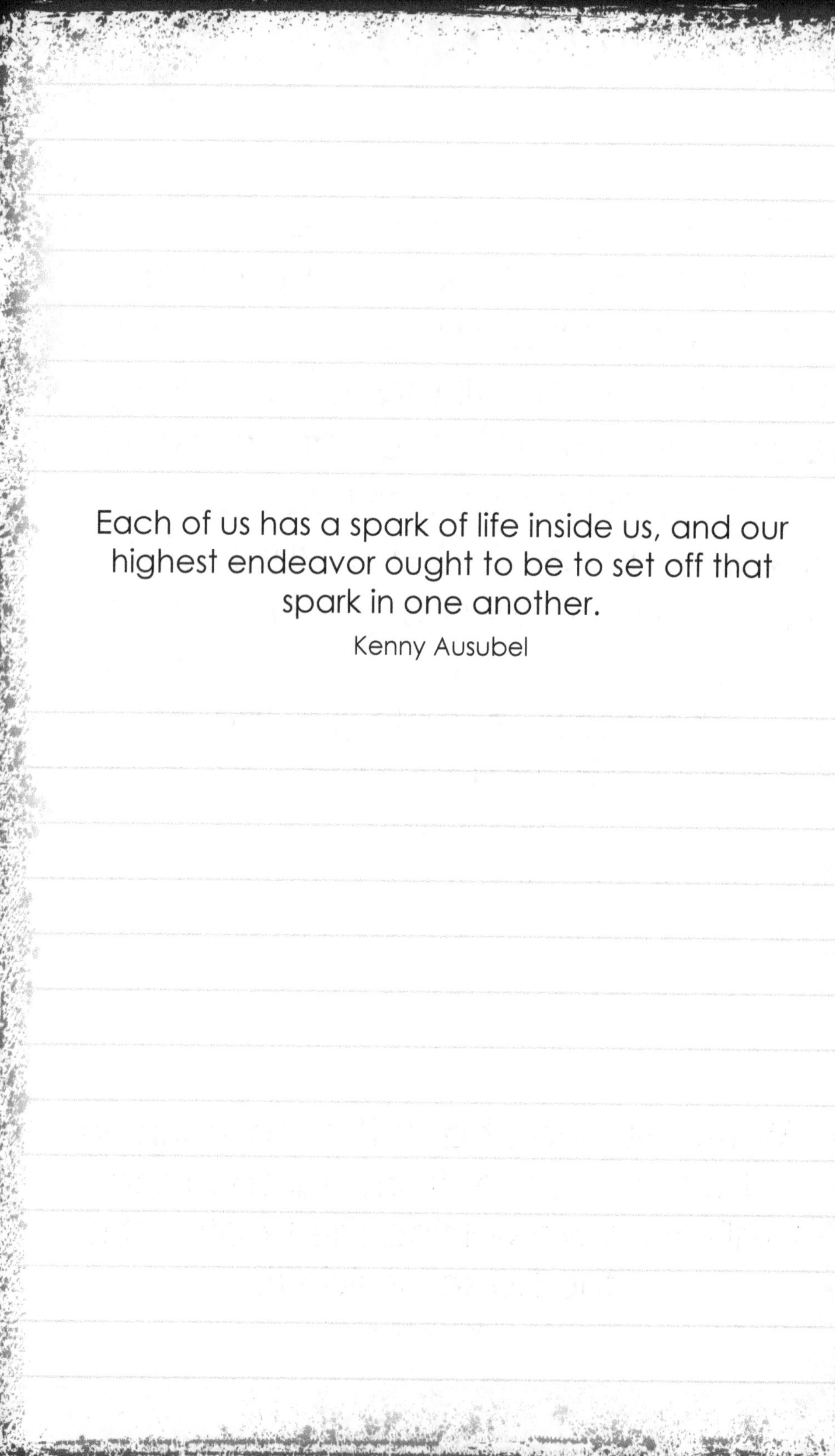
Each of us has a spark of life inside us, and our
highest endeavor ought to be to set off that
spark in one another.
Kenny Ausubel

A good laugh heals a lot of hurts.

A good laugh is sunshine in the house.

A smile is a curve that sets everything straight.
Phyllis Diller

A smile starts on the lips, a grin spreads to the eyes,
a chuckle comes from the belly; but a good laugh
bursts forth from the soul, overflows,
and bubbles all around.

Carolyn Birmingham

A well-balanced person is one who finds both
sides of an issue laughable.
Herbert Procknow

Against the assault of laughter, nothing can stand.
Mark Twain

Always laugh when you can.

It is cheap medicine.

Lord Byron

Among those whom I like or admire, I can find no
common denominator, but among those whom I love,
I can: all of them make me laugh.

W. H. Auden

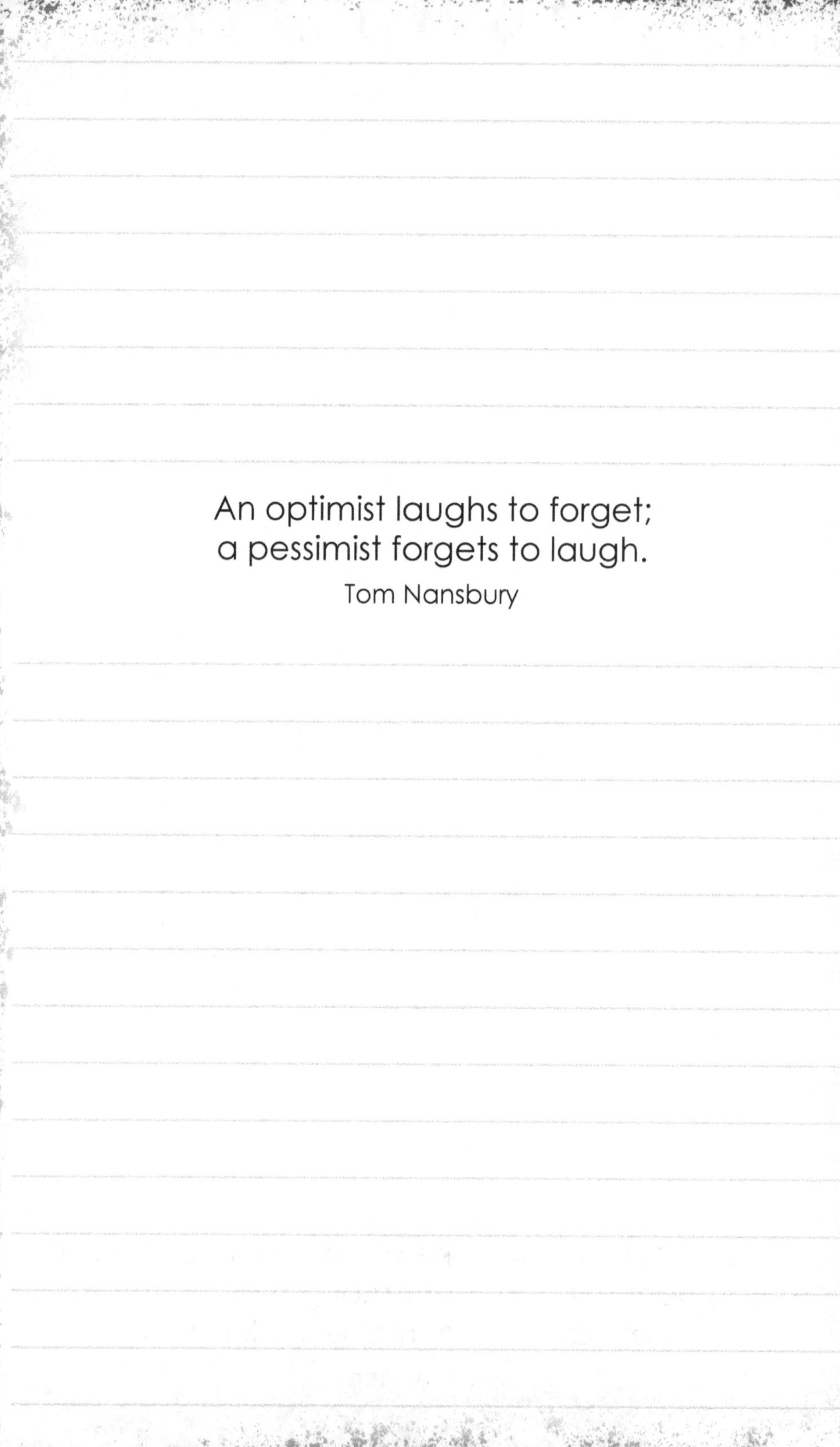
An optimist laughs to forget;
a pessimist forgets to laugh.
Tom Nansbury

And we should consider every day lost on which we
have not danced at least once. And we should
call every truth false which was not accompanied
by at least one laugh.

Friedrich Nietzsche

As soap is to the body, so laughter is to the soul.
A Jewish Proverb

A real friend is one who walks in when the
rest of the world walks out.

Walter Winchell

Grim care, moroseness, and anxiety—all this rust of life
ought to be scoured off by the oil of mirth.
Mirth is God's medicine.

Henry Ward Beecher

Humor is a prelude to faith and
laughter is the beginning of prayer.
Reinhold Niebuhr

Humor is laughing at what you haven't got
when you ought to have it.
James Langston Hughes

I have always felt that laughter in the face of reality
is probably the finest sound there is and will last
until the day when the game is called on account
of darkness. In this world, a good time to laugh
is any time you can.

Linda Ellerbee

I have not seen anyone dying of laughter, but I know millions who are dying because they are not laughing.

Dr. Madan Kataria

I never would have made it if I could not have laughed. It lifted me momentarily out of this horrible situation, just enough to make it livable.

Viktor Frankl - Asuchwitz survivor

If Laughter cannot solve your
problems, it will definitely DISSOLVE your problems; so
that you can think clearly what to do about them.
Dr. Madan Kataria

Laughing is, and always will be, the best
form of therapy.
Dau Voire

If you are happy and people around you are not happy, they will not allow you to stay happy. Therefore much of our happiness depends upon our ability to spread happiness around us.

Dr. Madan Kataria

You don't stop laughing because you grow older. You grow older because you stop laughing.
Maurice Chavelier

If you have no tragedy, you have no comedy. Crying
and laughing are the same emotion. If you laugh too
hard, you cry. And vice versa.

Sid Caesar

If you would not be laughed at, be the first to
laugh at yourself.
Benjamin Franklin

Laugh my friend, for laughter ignites a fire within the pit of your belly and awakens your being.

Stella & Blake

Laughter connects you with people. It's almost impossible to maintain any kind of distance or any sense of social hierarchy when you're just howling with laughter. Laughter is a force for democracy.

John Cleese

Laughter has no foreign accent.
Paul Lowney

Laughter is God's hand on the
shoulder of a troubled world.
Bettenell Huntznicker

Laughter is the shortest distance between two people.

Victor Borge

Laughter is the sun that drives winter from
the human face.

Victor Hugo

Laughter lets me relax. It's the equivalent of taking a deep breath, letting it out and saying, 'This, too, will pass'.

Odette Pollar

Let your heart by merry. A merry heart is
like a medicine.
Yhe Bible

Life does not cease to be funny when people die any more than it ceases to be serious when people laugh.

George Bernard Shaw

Life is a great big canvas;
throw all the paint on it you can.
Danny Kaye

Mirth is like a flash of lightning that breaks through
a gloom of clouds and glitter for the moment.
Cheerfulness keeps up daylight in the mind, filling it
with steady and perpetual serenity.

Samuel Johnson

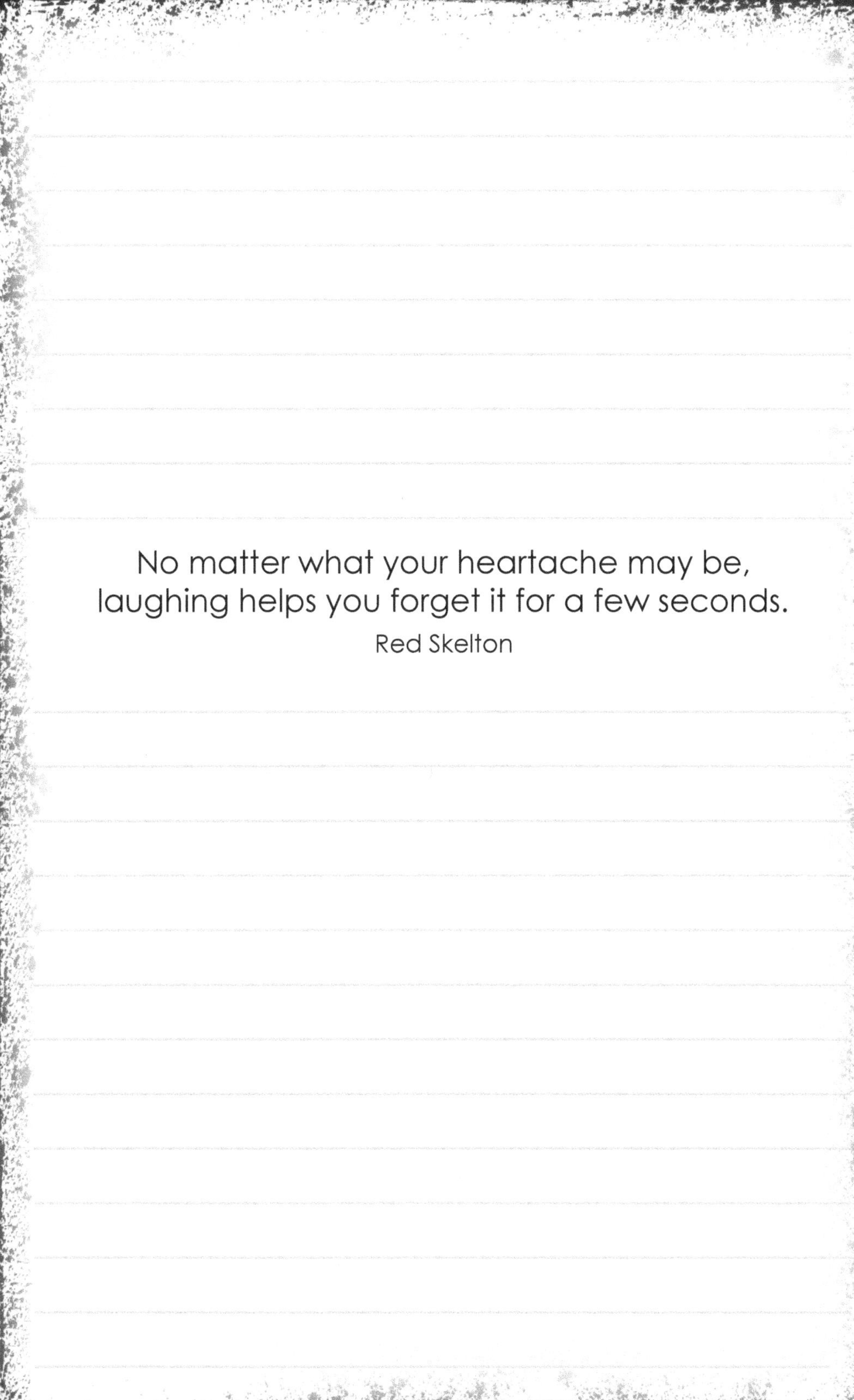

No matter what your heartache may be,
laughing helps you forget it for a few seconds.
Red Skelton

The best way to cheer yourself is to try to
cheer someone else up.
Mark Twain

The person who can bring the spirit of laughter
into a room is indeed blessed.
Bennett Cerf

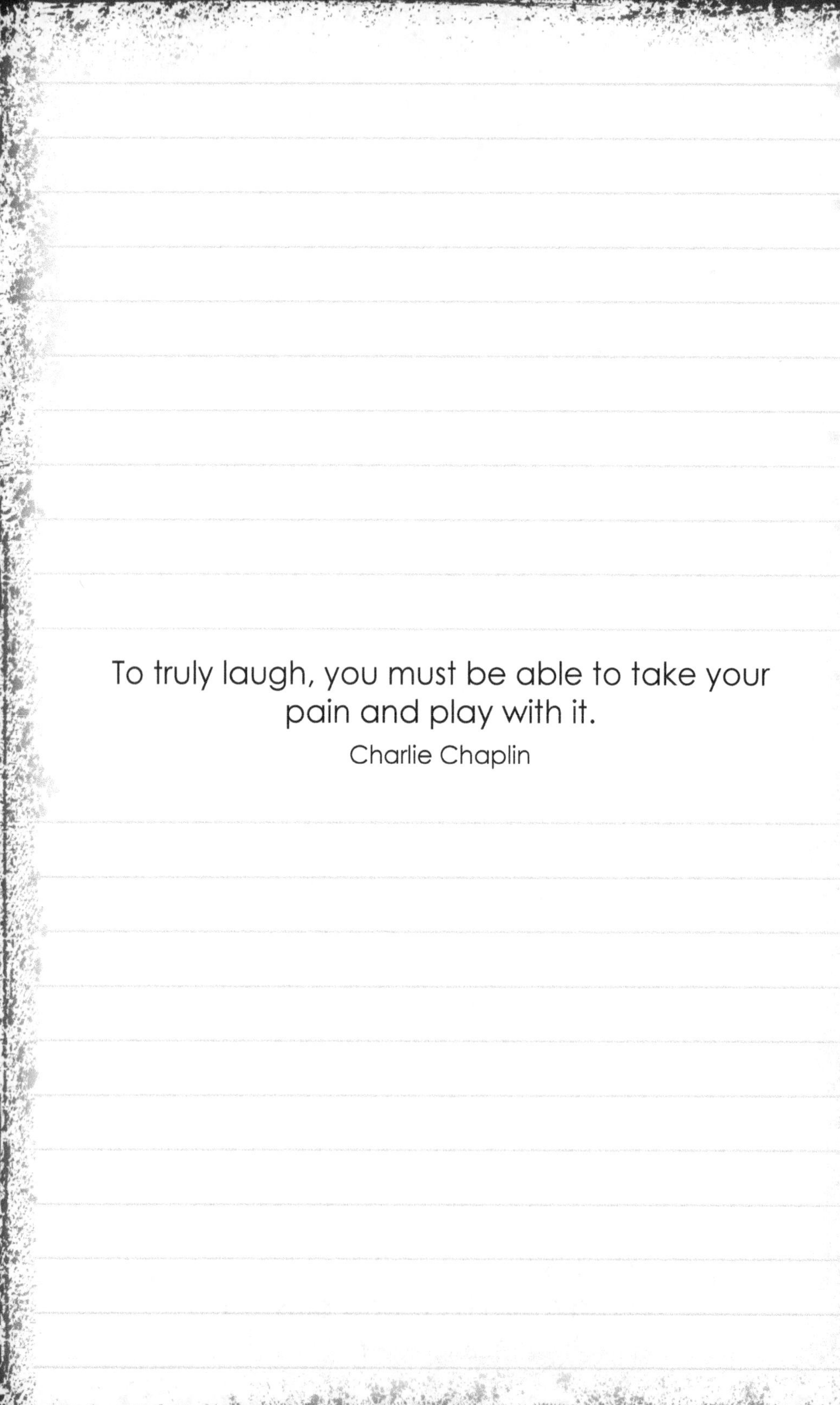
To truly laugh, you must be able to take your pain and play with it.
Charlie Chaplin

When you laugh, you get a glimpse of God.
Merrily Belgum

Wit is the key, I think, to anybody's heart,
because who doesn't like to laugh?
Julia Roberts

With mirth and laughter let old wrinkles come.
William Shakespeare

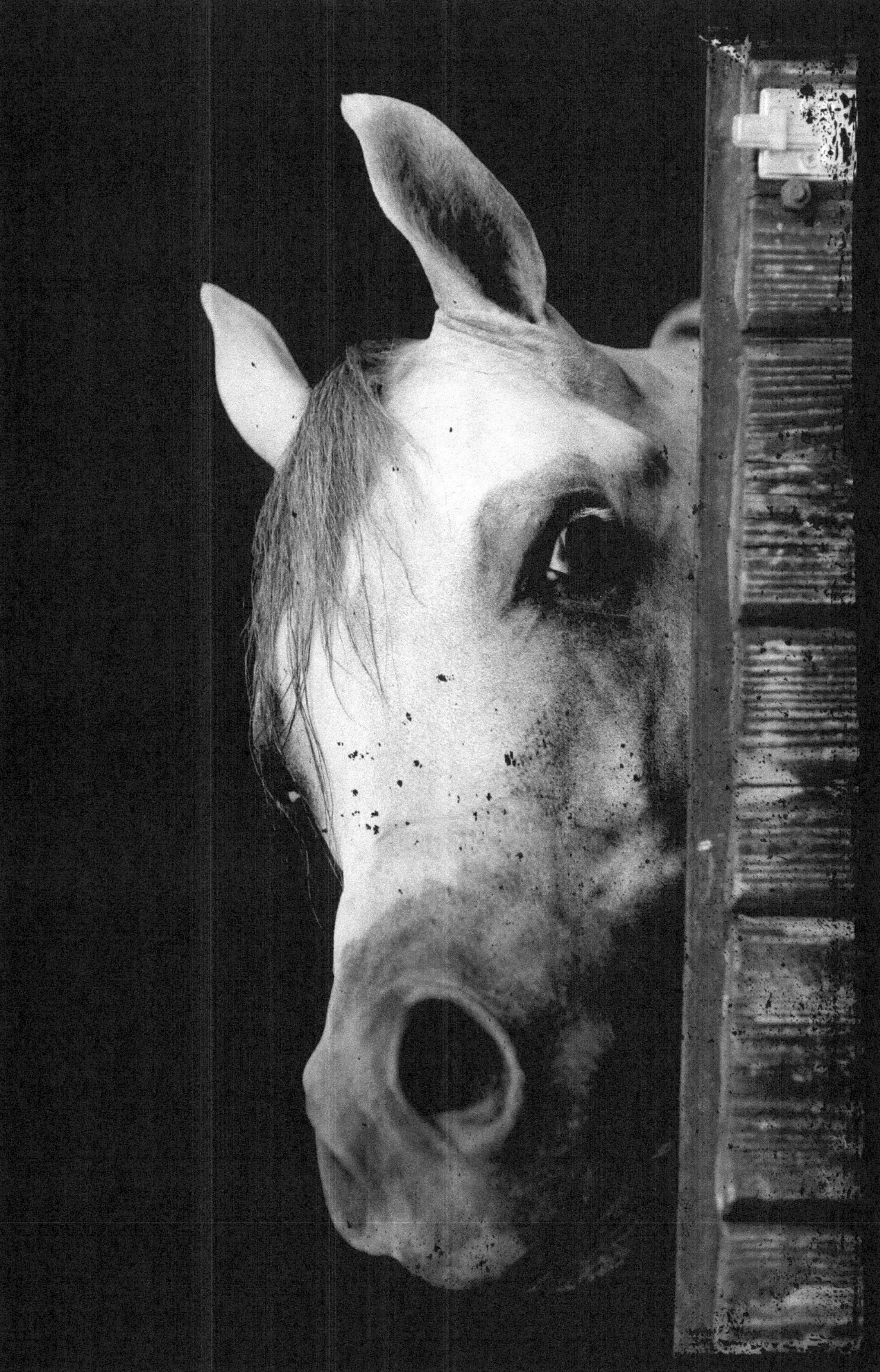

Your joy is your sorrow unmasked.
And the self-same well from which your laughter
rises was oftentimes fill ed with your tears.
Kahlil Gibran

Your body cannot heal without play. Your mind cannot heal without laughter. Your soul cannot heal without joy.

Catherine Rippenger Fenwick

Laughter is a sense of proportion and a power
of seeing yourself from the outside.

Zero Mostel

Laughter is an instant vacation.

I love people who make me laugh.
Audrey Hepburn

It was the way you laughed ...
I knew I wanted that in my life.
R.M. Drake

There is nothing in the world so irresistibly contagious
as laughter and good humor.
Charles Dickens

If you want to tell people the truth, make them laugh, otherwise they'll kill you.

George Bernard Shaw

And we should consider every day lost on which we
have not danced at least once. And we should call
every truth false which was not accompanied by at
least one laugh. Laughter is wine for the soul - laughter
soft, or loud and deep, tinged through with seriousness
- the hilarious declaration made by man
that life is worth living.

Sean O'Casey

What a Beautiful Horse
Jo's Journey

Even as a child growing up in the Cariboo of Beautiful British Columbia, Canada, Jo loved horses, cowboys and all things country. She was an avid rider who felt comfortable in the ranching lifestyle. Looking back, she could have been a rancher's wife pursuing the western way of life that she loved.

Life has a way of surprizing us, so when Jo was called to the Mission Field in Bolivia some thirty-three years ago, everything changed. Jo's journey has been incredibly rewarding as she grew to love Bolivia and the people there. She adopted children who now have their own children, (Jo's grandchildren) all while living a life of service to God.

Jo has never lost her love and passion for horses and because of that she has created her popular face book page and website called 'What a Beautiful Horse', to share her love of horses with others. Jo and 'What a Beautiful Horse' have touched the lives and heart strings of thousands with stunning horse pictures depicting every breed and color. The inspirational quotes and sayings, some of them showing Jo's wonderful sense of humor, relate to our everyday lives and put smiles on our faces. You are invited to come along for the ride.

Sandy Smith
Friend and horse enthusiast
November 2019

Other journals by Jo:
WHAT A BEAUTIFUL HORSE